ARCHITECTURE AND THE AMBIENT

ARCHITECTURE AND THE AMBIENT

MARIO BOTTA

EDITED AND WITH AN EPILOGUE BY MARKUS BREITSCHMID

TRANSLATED BY ALICE FRANCESCONI AND MARIANNA GALBUSERA
WITH THE ASSISTANCE OF MARKUS BREITSCHMID

VIRGINIA TECH ARCHITECTURE PUBLICATIONS

Architecture and the Ambient
Mario Botta
Volume 2 of Series Texts on *Architectura et ars*

Editor: Markus Breitschmid
Epilogue and Biographical Information: Markus Breitschmid
Translation from Italian to English: Alice Francesconi, Marianna Galbusera with the
Assistance of Markus Breitschmid

Originally published in Italian as:
Architettura e ambiente. Note per una conferenza di Mario Botta
Author: Mario Botta
In: Mario Botta 1978-1982. Il laboratorio di architettura / Milano / Electa Editrice /
1983 / pp. 115-116.

Virginia Tech Architecture Publications
Blacksburg, Virginia 24061
United States of America
Phone: +1-540-231-5383
Internet: www.archdesign.vt.edu

Printed in the United States of America

Texts on Architecture & Art Series

The intent of the series 'Texts on Architecture & Art' is to make important texts on architecture and art originally published in other languages available to an English-speaking readership. Each volume consists of a first-time English translation of a text on architecture or art. The series is dedicated to the understanding of theoretical problems of architecture and art.

Series Editor: Markus Breitschmid

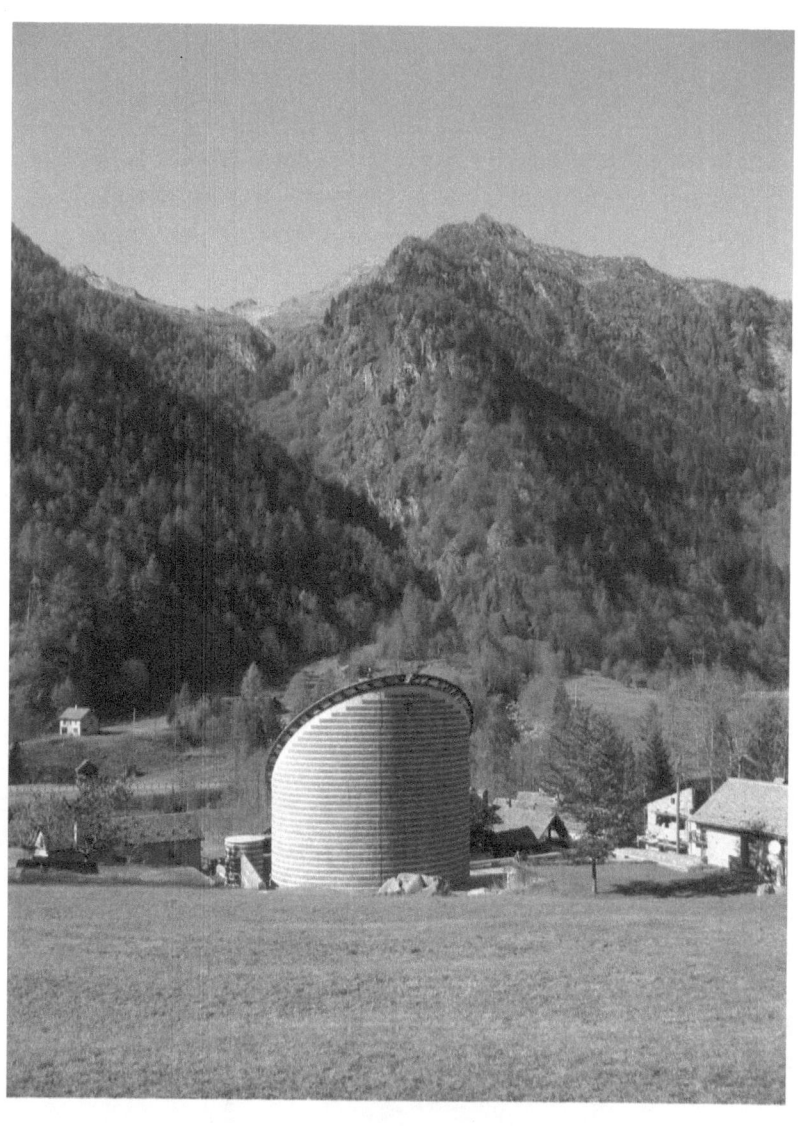

CHURCH OF SAN GIOVANNI BATTISTA
MOGNO, TICINO, SWITZERLAND
1996-1998
ARCHITECT: MARIO BOTTA

ARCHITECTURE AND THE AMBIENT

NOTES FOR A CONFERENCE

THE ORIGINAL EDITION OF THE TEXT PRESENTED IN THIS VOLUME IS TITLED *ARCHITETTURA E AMBIENTE - NOTE PER UNA CONFERENZA DI MARIO BOTTA*. IT WAS WRITTEN BY MARIO BOTTA. THE TEXT WAS ORIGINALLY PUBLISHED IN THE BOOK *MARIO BOTTA 1978-1982 - IL LABORATORIO DI ARCHITETTURA* IN 1983.

[FOREWORD]

This article addresses some issues occurring directly in my research and in my work as an architect.

Therefore these are observations of a practitioner, not of a critic or an historian: these are observations accrued through empirical research that feeds and limits my way of "making architecture." This is a work still in progress, limited in time, which has to be considered heterogeneous and anecdotal, like an architect's research and operational work is nowadays.

For this reason, it is difficult for me to estimate my work's intentions and prospects beyond the themes elaborated in the single items and the single experiences with a more general critical synthesis to enable and justify possible theorization. So these notes should be understood as annotations of some recurrent themes in my current research.

In spite of this, today I consider it useful to discuss in this essay some of my experiences.

I believe that for us architects it is legitimate and thus not too ambitious to talk about and discuss the issues and the meaning adopted nowadays by architecture, including through the limited testimony of our own experiences.

In this way misunderstandings and ambiguities will be laid open. The most direct discussion will have the merit of being expressly "my own" as is proper for a mainly creative activity.

In this case the relations between architecture and its "environment" and the search for the meanings that they assume nowadays will be an opportunity to discuss what I now believe and feel about some aspects of this discipline.

It is perhaps worthwhile, in order to better understand the meaning of the following comments, to make clear the difference between these two possible interpretations.

[A.] What I think about architecture constitutes the whole set of ideas and thoughts that nowadays I assume as theoretical foundations, drawn from the broader theorization of the subject.

It is all the culture and the knowledge that the time I live in can offer me. In a certain sense it represents the collective cultural heritage handed down to us by the previous generations. These thoughts and interpretations have influenced my development. In other words they constitute the theoretical condition of being an architect nowadays, a direct or indirect heir of what the previous architectural research has produced.

In a whole sense these are the aspects that are rational and describable enough to constitute the social and collective value of the discipline, around which a rational critical analysis is possible.

[B.] What I feel about architecture instead involves the most subjective and autobiographical aspects. In a certain way these are the most hidden in that they constitute the irrational motivations (sometimes hardly describable) that also take part in the process of the evaluation and the choices that characterize the act of projecting and making a project.

These notes continually switch between these two modes (collective and private, rational and irrational).

ARCHITECTURE AND THE AMBIENT

Every work of architecture has its own ambient.

This [the ambient] for convenience can be defined as its territory.

Between architecture and territory exists a continuous relationship of mutual dependence that is established from the first moments of projection.

The first act of "making architecture" is that of taking account of its territory. Its interpretation, the reading of the territory, occurs through the verifications and relationships that are defined through the choices made in the project.

The relationship between architecture and territory is not static.

It is a dynamic and continuous relationship that is specified through the project's process and that is consolidated in a new balance at the moment of the realization of the architectural work. Then, after the realization, this relationship becomes dynamic again and continually defines changing relationships with the architectonic work. In a certain sense it can be said that the territory is in continuous dialog with its own architecture, not unlike the changing of time and history.

The architectural work specifies and defines itself over time, proposing itself as a model of its own habitat by consolidating and assuming the new meanings of its context.

Between architecture and ambient (whether built or natural) there is therefore a real relationship of mutual and continuous exchange (giving — getting).

I believe that the quality of every architectural act directly depends on the intensity of this exchange.

Regarding architecture, I do not love the object as such, but the relationships (spatial, emotional, etc.) that the object is able to establish with its own ambient.

It is around this relationship and in the insistence of gathering its meanings, that, with a hierarchy of priorities, I develop my research, my way of making and interpreting architecture.

It is in the evaluation of these relationships that nowadays I always turn my interest when reading and interpreting an architectural work.

In order to better understand the nature and the meaning of these relationships, I think it is useful to make some observations on a few big misunderstandings that, today, subsist as generalized convictions and that I think might be the necessary condition for a corrected vision of these problems.

A misunderstanding that periodically re-emerges in the evaluation of the relationships between architecture and ambient is the idea that subordinates every new architectonic intervention under a presumed superiority of the values of the preexisting context.

In this perspective the territory is seen as the good that needs to be preserved and protected from the aggressions and the destructions inflicted on the existing conditions by the new interventions. This is a very widespread attitude (on which the numerous groups and societies of environmental and landscape preservation and protection are based on) that interprets the

existing context and the environmental equilibrium as a static condition loaded with value.
Moreover – and this is not meant ironically –
these values are usually declared valuable and
discovered for the first time, just in time, when
a new architectonic intervention is imminent.

This is a widespread attitude that also influ-
ences a great many architects.

I believe that this attitude, rather than expressing sensitivity and attention toward existing
values, expresses fear and mistrust toward every new expression.

Most of the time, more than expressing an attitude of conservation, it expresses a reactionary
attitude.

This way of seeing the relationships between
architecture and its surroundings has directly

influenced the majority of existing building codes; it has not developed good "common sense" much either, nor has it hindered speculative uses of the land for buildings. Worse, most of the time, such a reactionary way of seeing the relationship between architecture and its surroundings is the accomplice of the speculative destruction of the land it seeks to protect.

From this perspective, it can be noticed how the protection of the values of the environment and of the landscape is often not entrusted to rational motivations, but to the most perverse aesthetical senses (of adaptation, of integration etc.) of the numerous protection and conservation commissions and associations, where the cultural corruption of these experts, judging by what has been produced in the last years, seems really not to have limits.

Contrary to this attitude, I think that, more simply, the evidence of the facts must be accepted, and, once the legitimacy of the intervention is recognized, it should be placed as the fulcrum of a new transformation. In such cases, architecture is qualified as an instrument of construction of a new balance where the existing values will be considered – yet not defended or protected irrationally and overzealously – in order to be interpreted and projected as values for new needs.

We should talk then, not about protection, but about promotion of the landscape's values and testimonies.

In this way many misunderstandings could be omitted, above all else, the illusions and phantoms of an impossible conservation. Rather, what I propose would give place to an analysis that is more honest, and therefore more committed to finding a new balance between men and his ambient.

From an analysis of the relations and the meanings that are defined between architecture and the ambient, I believe that three aspects take part constantly in the moment of evaluation and comparison during the design and planning process. These three aspects are:

[1.] The first aspect is the reading and the interpretation of the ambient as a physical fact.

The territory is seen then as a place, a particular "site", something unique, that is tightly linked to the geography and morphology of the context where we are called to work.

Around this physical fact originates the need for comprehending and defining the identity of this place, for the identification of its meanings and its own peculiar characteristics, to adopt as elements of reference and continuous dialogue with the architectural fact.

A plain, a forest, a lake, a hill, or a village, are then real elements of the new project. They are to be considered the meeting place between natural and artificial.

In this way every "territory" has its own character, its own depth, its own structure, its own law which has to be understood and adopted as a parameter that is sometimes hidden yet still meaningful for the new architecture.

Water and pilings, rock and stone masonry, clay and brick masonry are a series of binomials that still hide the deepest meaning of creating contact and possession between the man and his land.

[2.] The second aspect is the ambient's interpretation, as evidenced in history and memory.

This is an aspect that involves all that exceeds physical facts. What is referred to here include symbolic aspects, atavic efforts, as well as un-known conflicts that the earth hides, which come back as memory's facts in every new project. These are presences and values that we have, not as nostalgic projections of a past, but as facts of a real material, as presences of that work, or better yet, of the work's effort, which has brought us to our reality. The ambient is also and above all evidence of the presence of men and past generation that gives meaning and courage to our work.

[3.] A third aspect that is present in the relations between architecture and ambient is the notion of time.

A piece of architecture, as we said, has the power to make a place different today from what and how it was yesterday. It may be the tangible expression of man's work – man-made artifices – relating to his nature.

In this way architecture is changing and transforming itself in synchronization with its time.

The periodical relation with nature's laws (the seasonal cycle, the passing of the day, etc.) makes architecture a moment of continuous and dynamic reference with these "cosmic" values of our life.

I think that it is precisely in the comparison and awareness of these facts that architecture can be fed by its context. Then architecture as a formal expression of history will know how to be an active witness of the aspirations, of the concerns, and of the hopes of our culture.

Mario Botta

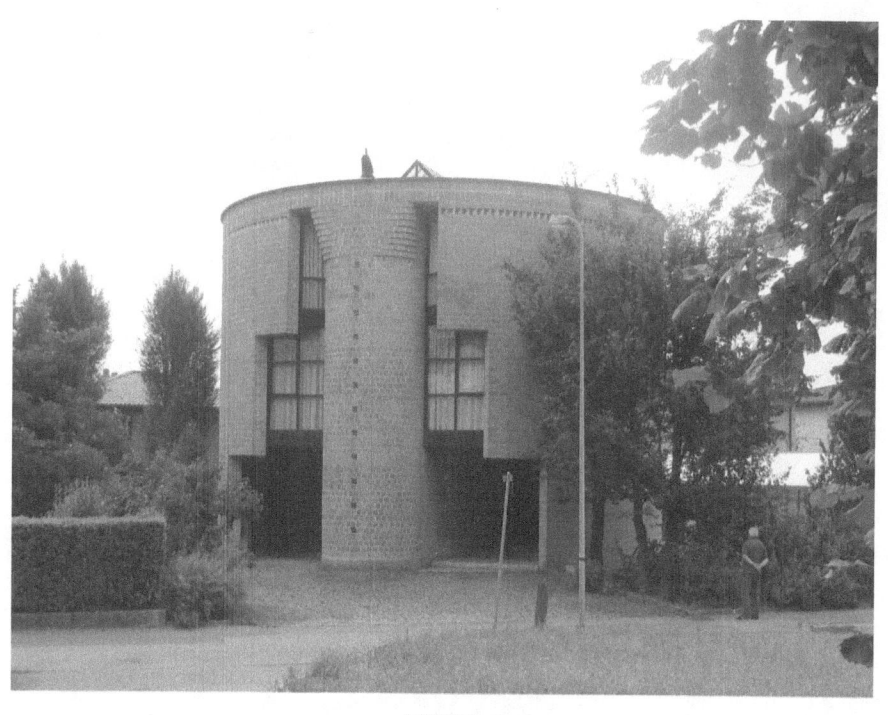

HOUSE
STABIO, TICINO, SWITZERLAND
1980
ARCHITECT: MARIO BOTTA

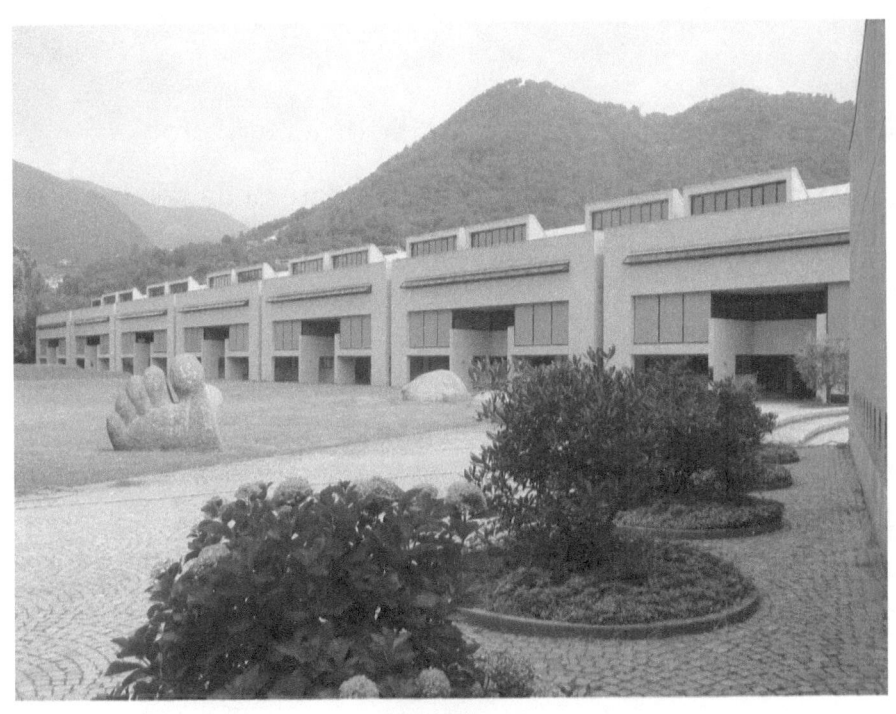

MIDDLE SCHOOL
MORBIO INFERIORE, TICINO, SWITZERLAND
1972-1977
ARCHITECT: MARIO BOTTA

ARCHITETTURA E AMBIENTE

NOTE PER UNA CONFERENZA

[PREFAZIONE]

Questa comunicazione tratta di alcuni problemi che intervengono direttamente nella mia ricerca e nel mio operare in quanto architetto.

Sono quindi osservazioni di un operatore diretto, non di un critico o di uno storico: sono osservazioni maturate nell'ambito di una ricerca empirica, di quella ricerca che alimenta e limita il mio modo di "fare architettura." Si tratta di un'attività ancora in corso nel suo svolgimento, limitata nel tempo, che dev'essere ritenuta eterogenea ed aneddotica, come è la ricerca e il lavoro operativo di un architetto oggi.

Per questo mi è difficile valutare le intenzioni e le prospettive del mio lavoro al di là dei temi elaborati nei singoli oggetti e delle singole esperienze con una sintesi critica più generale che permetta e che giustifichi una possibile teorizzazione. Converrà quindi interpretare queste note come appunti di alcuni temi ricorrenti nella mia attuale ricerca.

Malgrado ciò ho ritenuto utile discutere oggi qui talune mie esperienze.

Io credo che per noi architetti sia legittimo e quindi non troppo ambizioso parlare e discutere dei problemi e del significato che assume oggi l'architettura anche attraverso le testimonianze limitate delle proprie esperienze. In tal modo cadranno ambiguità e molti malintesi. La discussione più diretta avrà il merito di essere dichiaratamente "di parte" come conviene ad un'attività prevalentemente creativa.

In questo caso i rapporti tra architettura e il suo "environnement" e la ricerca dei significati che oggi assumono, saranno di pretesto per discutere su quanto oggi io penso e su quanto oggi io sento, rispetto a taluni aspetti della disciplina.

Conviene forse, per meglio capire il senso delle successive osservazioni, precisare la differenza di queste due possibili interpretazioni.

[A.] Che cosa io penso dell'architettura costituisce l'insieme delle idee e dei pensieri che oggi assumo come fondamenti teorici, distinguendo nella vasta teorizzazione che propone la disciplina.

È tutto quanto mi può offrire l'informazione e la cultura del mio tempo. In un certo senso rappresenta il patrimonio culturale collettivo trasmessoci dalle generazioni precedenti. Sono quei pensieri e quelle interpretazioni che hanno condizionato e alimentato la mia formazione. In altre parole costituiscono la condizione teorica dell'essere architetto oggi, direttamente o indirettamente erede di quanto prodotto dalla ricerca architettonica precedente.

Nel suo insieme sono gli aspetti sufficientemente razionali e descrivibili che costituiscono i valori sociali e collettivi della disciplina, sono quei valori attorno ai quali è possibile una valutazione critica ragionata.

[B.] Che cosa invece io sento rispetto all'architettura coinvolge gli aspetti più soggettivi, più autobiografici, in un certo senso più segreti che nel loro insieme costituiscono le motivazioni irrazionali (talvolta difficilmente descrivibili) che pure intervengono nel processo di valutazione e di scelte che caratterizzano un atto progettuale.

È nell'alternarsi di questi due momenti (collettivo e privato, razionale e irrazionale) che si collocano questi appunti.

ARCHITETTURA E AMBIENTE

Ogni opera di architettura ha un proprio ambiente.

Questo per comodità può essere definito come il suo territorio.

Fra architettura e territorio intercorre un rapporto continuo di reciproca dipendenza che viene ad instaurarsi fin dai primi momenti progettuali.

Il primo atto del "fare architettura" è la presa di conoscenza del suo territorio. La sua interpretazione, la sua lettura, avviene attraverso le verifiche e le relazioni che si vengono a definire con le scelte progettuali.

Il rapporto fra architettura e territorio non è un rapporto fisso.

È un rapporto dinamico e continuo che si precisa attraverso l'iter progettuale e che si consolida in un nuovo equilibrio al momento della realizzazione dell'opera architettonica. Poi, a realizzazione avvenuta, questo rapporto riprende ad essere dinamico e a definire con l'opera architettonica rapporti continuamente mutevoli. In un certo senso si può dire che il territorio dialoga con la propria architettura in modo continuo come il mutarsi del tempo e della storia.

Il lavoro di architettura si puntualizza e si definisce nel tempo col suo proporsi in quanto modello di habitat proprio con il consolidarsi e con l'assumere nuovi significati nel suo contesto.

Fra architettura e ambiente (costruito o naturale non importa) sussiste quindi un rapporto reale di scambio (dare-avere) reciproco e continuo.

Io credo che dalla intensità di questo scambio dipenda direttamente la qualità di ogni operazione architettonica.

Dell'architettura io amo non l'oggetto, ma le relazioni (quelle spaziali, emotive, ecc.) che questo oggetto riesce a stabilire con il proprio ambiente.

È attorno a questo rapporto, è nell'insistenza di coglierne i suoi significati, che si svolge, con una gerarchia prioritaria, la mia ricerca, il mio modo di fare e di interpretare l'architettura.

È nella valutazione di questi rapporti che sempre rivolgo l'interesse nella lettura e nell'interpretazione di un'opera di architettura oggi.

Per meglio capire la natura e il significato di questi rapporti, penso sia utile qualche osservazione su taluni grossi equivoci che sussistono come convinzioni generalizzate, oggi, e che mi sembra condizionino una corretta visione di questi problemi.

Un malinteso che periodicamente riemerge nella valutazione dei rapporti fra architettura e ambiente è l'idea che subordina ogni nuovo intervento architettonico ad una presunta superiorità dei valori del contesto preesistente.

In quest'ottica il territorio è visto come un bene da tutelare e da proteggere contro le aggressioni e le distruzioni attuate dai nuovi interventi. È un atteggiamento assai diffuso (sul quale si fondano le numerose società e i numerosi comitati di tutela: del paesaggio, dell'ambiente, ecc.) che interpreta il contesto esistente e l'equilibrio dell'ambiente come un elemento statico, carico di valori e di testimonianze il più della volte (e sia detto non ironicamente) emersi o riscoperti nell'imminenza e con lo stimolo del futuro pericolo (individuato nel nuovo intervento).

È un atteggiamento diffuso che condiziona anche gran parte degli architetti.

Io credo che questa attitudine piuttosto che esprimere sensibilità ed attenzione verso valori esistenti esprima paura e sfiducia verso ogni nuova espressione.

Il più delle volte più che esprimere un atteggiamento di conservazione esprime un'attitudine di reazione.

Questo modo di vedere i rapporti tra architettura e suo intorno ha direttamente influenzato la maggior parte della normativa edilizia esistente, ed ha condizionato non poco il comune "buon senso", senza tuttavia scalfire, ed anzi il più della volte rendendosi complice, la maggior parte delle operazioni speculative.

In quest'ottica si può notare come la tutela dei "valori" paesaggistici, ambientali ecc., sia spesso affidata non tanto a motivazioni razionali, ma ai più perversi sensi estetici (di ambientamento, di inserimento, ecc.) delle numerosissime commissioni e associazioni di protezione e di tutela dove la corruzione culturale di questi addetti ai lavori sembra veramente – a giudicare da quanto prodotto in questi ultimi anni – non avere limiti.

Contrariamente a questo atteggiamento io penso che più semplicemente si debba accettare l'evidenza dei fatti e, una volta riconosciuta la legittimità dell'intervento, porre lo stesso come fulcro di una nuova trasformazione. In tal caso l'architettura si qualifica come strumento di costruzione di un nuovo equilibrio dove i valori esistenti (naturali o costruiti) saranno assunti non per essere difesi o protetti, ma per essere interpretati e proiettati come valori nelle nuove esigenze.

Si dovrà parlare allora non di protezione ma di promozione per i valori e le testimonianze del paesaggio.

In tal modo molti equivoci vengono a cadere: le illusioni e i fantasmi di una conservazione impossibile potranno lasciare il posto ad una lettura più disincantata, e perciò più impegnata nello stabilire un nuovo equilibrio fra l'uomo e il suo ambiente.

Da un'analisi dei rapporti e dei significati che si definiscono tra architettura e ambiente credo che tre aspetti intervengano come costante nel momento di valutazione e di confronto durante il processo di progettazione.

[1.] Innanzitutto la lettura e l'interpretazione dell'ambiente, in quanto dato fisico.

Il territorio è visto allora come luogo, come "sito" particolare, qualcosa di unico strettamente legato alla geografia e alla morfologia del contesto nel quale si è chiamati ad intervenire.

È attorno a questo dato fisico che scaturisce l'esigenza per la comprensione e la definizione della identità di questo luogo, l'identificazione dei suoi significati e delle sue caratteristiche più proprie, da assumere come elementi di riferimento e di dialogo continuo con il dato architettonico.

Una pianura, un bosco, un lago, una collina, o un villaggio, sono allora elementi reali del nuovo progetto. Il luogo di incontro tra naturale e artificiale.

Così ogni "territorio" ha un proprio carattere, un proprio spessore, una propria struttura, una propria legge da capire e da assumere come parametro talvolta segreto ma profondo per la nuova architettura.

Acqua e palafitte, roccia e muratura di sassi, argilla e muratura di mattoni, sono una serie di binomi che nascondono ancora oggi il senso più profondo del prendere contatto e possesso fra l'uomo e la sua terra.

[2.] Il secondo aspetto è l'interpretazione dell'environnement, in quanto testimonianza di storia e di memoria.

È un aspetto che coinvolge tutto quanto va oltre i dati fisici. Sono allora gli aspetti simbolici, le ataviche fatiche, le lotte sconosciute che la terra nasconde, che rientrano come dati di memoria in ogni nuovo progetto. Sono presenze e valori che ci appartengono non come proiezioni nostalgiche di un passato ma come dati di un tessuto reale, come presenze di quel lavoro o meglio della fatica di quel lavoro, che ci ha portato alla nostra realtà. L'environnement è anche e soprattutto testimonianza di questa presenza di uomini e generazioni estinte, ma che danno significato e coraggio per il nostro operare.

[3.] Un terzo aspetto presente nei rapporti fra architettura e ambiente è la nozione di tempo.

Un'architettura, è stato detto, fa si che un luogo oggi sia ancora diverso da ieri. È forse l'espressione tangibile del rapportarsi del lavoro dell'uomo (l'artificiale) alla propria natura.

È in tal modo che l'architettura si modifica e si trasforma in sincronia con il proprio tempo.

Il periodico rapportarsi alle leggi della natura (il ciclo stagionale, il trascorrere della giornata, ecc.) pone l'architettura come momento di riferimento continuo e dinamico con quei valori "cosmici" del nostro vivere.

Credo che proprio nel confronto e nella consapevolezza di questi dati che il fatto architettonico può oggi trovare alimento dal suo contesto. Allora l'architettura in quanto espressione formale della storia saprà essere testimone attivo delle aspirazioni, delle inquietudini e delle speranze della nostra cultura.

Mario Botta

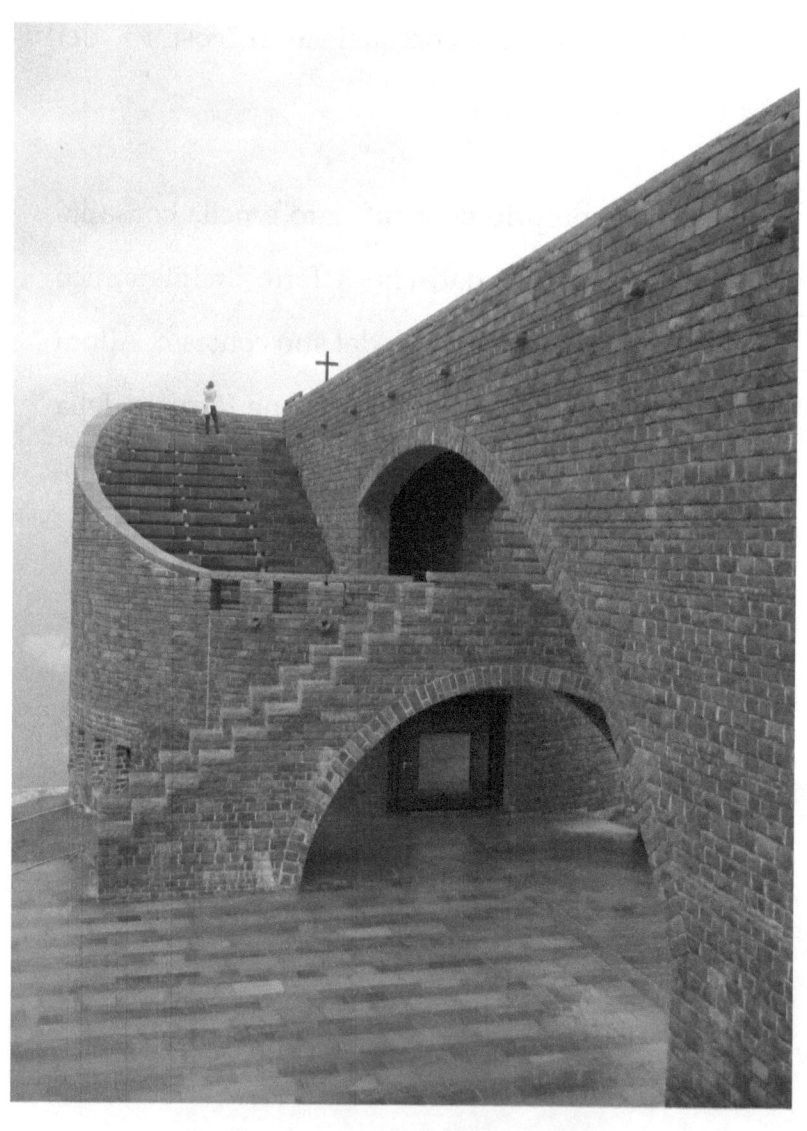

CHAPEL OF SANTA MARIA DEGLI ANGELI
MONTE TAMARO, TICINO, SWITZERLAND
1990-1996
ARCHITECT: MARIO BOTTA

EPILOGUE

BY MARKUS BREITSCHMID

It is not the aim of this epilogue to supply the first-time English translation of Mario Botta's less than 2000-word essay with a lengthy *exegesis*. An exegesis is a critical explanation or interpretation of a text. Rather, the epilogue is limited to a basic description of the text. However, to keep the epilogue in a descriptive mode should not be viewed that there is not plenty to consider in the essay titled *Architecture and the Ambient*. To limit the epilogue to a straightforward description is much more driven by the intention of how the series *Architectura et Ars* should serve further scholarship. The aim of the series is to present translations of important texts on architecture and art having not yet been available to a English-language readership and make them available for subsequent scholarship and, therefore, invite for their adaptation and interpretation by the readers in a largely 'unadulterated' way. In that spirit, the epilogue chooses to make only few remarks and comments to give the reader some orientation to situate the text when it seems necessary. With this self-imposed limitation in mind, the epilogue supplies a description of *Architecture and the Ambient* and is pointing to some pertinent references on which the text might be based on, and in whose ideational and historical relationship it stands. Other than those few remarks, the text by Mario Botta stands on its own feet.

Before delving into the essay, a few things should be pointed out about the translation of the essay. It turned out that the very title of the essay – *Architettura e ambiente* – posed the most discussion among the translators and the consulted English and Italian language experts. The first attempt to translate the essay resulted in the title *Architecture and the Environment* but it became evident that the English term environment has a different connotation than the Italian *ambiente,* particularly in the way Mario Botta uses it in his text. Ultimately it was decided to use the relatively uncommon English noun *ambient* for the translation. However, the noun ambient – while at some point related to each other – should not be confused with the very common word *ambiance* and its connotations. Used as a noun the word ambient defines an environment in a more encompassing way than the popular word environment. Beyond the prevalent physical, geographic, atmospheric, biological, and climatic connotation of the common understanding of environment today, heightened further by means of its strong association with the current understanding of nature, the ambient also encompasses a notion of context, of milieu, of locale, place, surroundings, terrain, setting, habitat, as well as genealogical and cultural backgrounds. From Botta's own text we can surmise that the identification of the most correct terminology is not solely a problem of the translation of the Italian original into English language. Botta himself did not seem to find a term in the Italian language that fully describes what he wanted it to define. As a consequence of the seeming lack of affinity, Botta invokes the word *territorio* [territory] to help describe the Italian term *ambiente*. He defines ambiente with: *"Questo per comodità può essere definito come il suo territorio* [The ambient for convenience can be defined as its territory]." As we will learn in Botta's essay, territory, from the Latin *territorium*, literally meaning the land around a town, is not only defined as geographic area, but also as a field of knowledge, and therefore, possesses that "collective cultural heritage" that is key for Botta's architectural conception.

Architettura e ambiente appeared first as an epilogue for the book *Mario Botta 1978-1982: Il laboratorio di architettura* but because it is subtitled with *note per una conferenza* [Notes for a conference] it can be assumed that it was initially written for the purpose of a lecture.[1] The essay is not dated. An inquiry with the office of Mario Botta, and a search of the archive by the staff of the office respectively, did not bring forward an exact date when the essay was written.

The essay has been translated into German in order to serve as a sort of frontispiece for the German edition of the book mentioned above.[2] It was titled

[1] Botta, Mario. "Architettura e ambiente. Note per una conferenza di Mario Botta," in: Pierluigi Nicolin; Francois Chaslin. *Mario Botta 1978-1982. Il laboratorio di architettura*. Milano: Electa Editrice 1983, pp.115-116

[2] Botta, Mario. "Die Bedeutung des Ortes in der Architektur. Notizen für einen Vortrag," in: Pierluigi Nicolin. *Mario Botta. Bauten und Projekte*. Stuttgart: Deutsche Verlags-Anstalt GmbH 1984, pp.13-15

Mario Botta: Bauten und Projekte and appeared one year after the Italian edition. While the book (with somewhat expanded content in the German edition in terms of the buildings presented if compared to the original Italian edition) also appeared in an English edition under the title of *Mario Botta. Buildings and projects 1961-1982,* largely mirroring the German edition, a translation of Botta's text was – strangely enough – not included.[3]

It is certainly more than noteworthy that this text only now becomes available for an English readership. This is particularly puzzling because the text – while brief in terms of word count – supplies at least one more explanation of what very well might be Mario Botta's most famous statement on architecture, namely, that "[t]he architectonic intervention is not an opportunity to build AT A PLACE but the artifact to BUILD A PLACE ..."[4] Of course, this statement by Botta was part of the accompanying catalog for the landmark exhibition *Tendenzen – Neuere Architektur im Tessin [Ten-*

[3] Nicolin, Pierluigi. *Mario Botta. Building and projects 1961-1982.* New York: Rizzoli 1984

[4] Mario Botta quoted in: Martin Steinmann. "Wirklichkeit als Geschichte. Stichworte zu einem Gespräch über Realismus in der Architektur," in: Martin Steinmann; Thomas Boga (eds.), *Tendenzen - Neuere Architektur im Tessin,* Zürich: gta 1975, p. 24

denza – Recent Architecture in the Ticino] held at the Swiss Federal Institute of Technology in Zurich, Switzerland, late in the year of 1975. It was that exhibition that proliferated the distinct approach to architecture practiced by numerous architects from the Italian-speaking Ticino region of Switzerland, including Mario Botta, to subsequent international prominence. Given the fact that the famed British historian and theoretician Kenneth Frampton made Botta's approach of "building the site" a key example in his seminal essay *Towards a Critical Regionalism*,[5] and thus further stimulated the propagation of the ideas of Botta's architecture in the Anglo-Saxon world, it is indeed surprising to learn that nobody saw value in translating *Architettura e ambiente* into English in the past thirty years. Therefore, the primary value of this volume is to make the text available for an English readership as a part of historiography, and to make it available for re-examination by the architectural discipline and profession.

[5] Frampton, Kenneth. "Towards a Critical Regionalism: Six points for an architecture of resistance," in: Hal Foster. *Anti-Aesthetic. Essay on Postmodern Culture.* Townsend, WA: Bay Press, 1983. Here quoted from the reprint by First New Press, New York, 1998, p.26

The structure of *Architecture and the Ambient* consists of a brief introductory part that could be considered a foreword, and then another, and only slightly longer part, that could be considered as the main part, containing the programmatic aspects of the essay. It is somewhat curious that Mario Botta used the identical title of the essay one more time to headline the main part, but it is reasonable to assume the intention for doing so is to establish a clear structural distinction between the introductory foreword and the following main body of the short essay.

With the foreword, Mario Botta stresses how he wants the text to be understood. He emphasizes from the outset that the text addresses "some issues occurring directly in my research and in my work as an architect." Botta pleads for modest expectations when he labels these issues he wants to address in the text as "observations of a practitioner, not of a critic or a historian" and he points out that they are the result of "empirical research that feeds and limits my way of 'making architecture'." He also reminds the reader that the outcomes have "to be considered heterogeneous and anecdotal" and less so "a more general critical synthesis to enable and justify possible theorization." However, while Botta labels his "observations of a practitioner" as "annotations," he clearly sees them as "legitimate and thus not too ambitious to talk about." Hence, Botta does ultimately aim for theorization when he wants to "discuss the issues and the meaning adopted nowadays by architecture." Botta states that it is through these attempts of theorization of one's own work that "misunderstandings and ambiguities will be laid open," recalling the importance of theoretical introspection needing to be given to one's own practical work.

The remaining part of the introductory foreword is divided into a section dealing with "What I think about architecture" and another section focused on "What I feel about architecture." Botta, here, attempts to construct the often-difficult bridge between so-called rational judgments and aesthetic judgments with which an architect is continuously engaged with. From this important distinction we can infer that Botta seems to accept or even embrace these dual tenants of modern aesthetics, as they have been formalized for the first time in the philosophical discourse of German Idealism.

Indeed, Botta's architectural conception issued in his essay is testimony to a complex theoretical background also steeped in a multi-facetted philosophical discourse, as it is witnessed by the adaptation and reformulation of some of those idealist tenants by a group of Northern Italian architects, historians, theoreticians, and critics, such as Manfredo Tafuri (1935–1994), Aldo Rossi (1931–1997), and Vittorio Gregotti (*1927), in whose haze Botta stands from an intellectual point of view. However, Botta does not discuss these dual tenants in lofty philosophical terms, but in direct practical application to his way of making architecture. Still, according to Botta, the first section "constitutes the whole set of ideas and thoughts that nowadays I assume as theoretical foundations, drawn from the broader theorization of the subject." Mario Botta understands this to be "all the culture and knowledge that the time I live in can offer me" and he points out that this "represents the collective cultural heritage handed down to us by the previous generations." Botta argues, "What I think about architecture" is "rational and describable enough" so that "a rational critical analysis is possible." On the other hand, "What I feel about architecture," for Botta, "involves the most subjective and auto-biographical aspects ... that also take part in the process of the evaluation and the choices that characterize the act of conceiving and making a project." Therefore, epistemologically, Mario Botta's knowledge base is not pure and dogmatic but rather heterogeneous and situated within the wide field of theories taken from idealism, rationalism, empiricism, and constructivism.

While it is not new what Botta says in this first part, he must have viewed it important enough to pre-amble his later observations with this general positioning of how he views his work as an architect. If nothing else, to position his conception of architecture on the two legs – "What I think about architecture" and "What I feel about architecture" –, as he does, suggests from the outset of approaching this essay (and by extension Botta's entire œuvre) not as the work of a rationalist alone, the often highly geometricized formal vocabulary of his buildings notwithstanding.

It is perhaps also the wisdom of Mario Botta that he knows the field of architecture to be multi-facetted that lets him appear to be careful with too dogmatic of a declaration. In any case, compared with the succinctness of the main part of the essay, the introductory foreword of *Architecture and the Ambient* has a somewhat rambling character. But it is not suggested that the opening part of the text is rambling in the sense of confusing or long-windedness but, again, rather in the sense of an architect who wants to set out a common understanding that architecture is complex in its conception and its justification. The setting of a complex ground for the conception of architecture becomes evident in the essay when Botta mercilessly criticizes the "very widespread attitude" by "numerous protection societies and associations … that interprets the existing context and the territorial equilibrium as a static element" and he thus suggests that architecture is often dealt with in too simplistic terms. Botta places these warning words not only toward governmental agencies but equally toward architects.

The main part of the essay begins with the most axiomatic sentence of the essay. It reads: "Every work of architecture has its own ambient." This dictum can be understood as an extension of the aforementioned famous quote by the architect in which he differentiates the constructing OF A PLACE with the building AT A PLACE. It is in the main part of the essay in which Botta provides an explanation of the difference between the two.

Before he describes the architectonic intervention as an "artifact to build a place," Botta makes two other arguments to help buttress his position. First, Botta chooses to view the territory as having a "continuous dialog with its own architecture, not unlike the changing of time and history." It is in a sentence like this one in which the affinity of the Italianate Botta with the theoretical thrust of Tafuri, Rossi and Gregotti becomes apparent. This kinship is discernable not only in assigning architecture a fundamental social role, a position that Botta does not explicitly address in political or sociological terms but much more so in the also shared neo-rationalist concern for the pivotal role of the historical continuum for the workings of the phenomenal world.

While these Italian theoreticians – with whose thoughts Botta was confronted with either through the channels of the *Istituto Universitario di Architettura di Venezia*, the university he studied at, or through their writings, particularly through the texts published in the prestigious Milano-based journal *Casabella* – accept Hegelian undercurrents for the basic mechanism that provides their historicity its dynamism, they do not follow a teleological scheme in which inevitable events succeed another in linear sequence. Instead, the school of thought of the so-called "School of Venice" advocates for an understanding of a continuous struggle played out on critical, theoretical and ideological levels, as well as, with regard to the discipline of architecture, through the multiple constraints placed on architectural practice. Mario Botta stresses the multitude of physical and non-physcial constraints that he views as important for his dynamic conception of architecture and the territory.

Still, Botta describes in very succinct terms how his historical model of understanding the currents that drive architecture is supposed to work: "Between architecture and territory exists a continuous relationship of mutual dependence that is established from the first moments of projection." And he lapidarily exclaims: "The relationship between architecture and territory is not static." Botta follows that assertion with a beautifully formulated description of how architecture and territory stay in a continuous dialog, not unlike the historical fluidity of time:

> "It is a dynamic and continuous relationship that is specified through the project's process and that is consolidated in a new balance at the moment of the realization of the architectural work. Then, after the realization, this relationship becomes dynamic again and continually defines changing relationships with the architectonic work ... The architectural work specifies and defines itself over time, proposing itself as a model of its own habitat by consolidating and assuming the new meanings of its context."

For Mario Botta, it is the "intensity of this exchange," the exchange between the continuously changing meanings of architecture and the ambient, on which depends "the quality of every architectural act."

Also very influential for Mario Botta is the "School of Venice"-theoreticians' understanding that the continuous historical struggle continuous in the present time. Therefore, history in general and architecture history in particular is not a dead antiquarian subject, but an open arena for discourse. It was maybe Aldo Rossi who made the most deliberate statements in that regard. For Rossi, this meant that architecture could be made subject to history, not an antiquarian kind of history, but with the aim to historicize architecture in order to bring about new theories for architecture – and this is important – from architecture itself. Instead of deducing architecture from extra-architectural sources as it had become widespread among architects in the late 1960s (in order to supposedly correct the mistakes of architectural modernism), Rossi articulated a believable basis for the autonomy of architecture and thus for the reaffirmation of architecture itself, arguably the most important theoretical outcome of Italian Neo-rationalism. The continued historicizing that is key to Rossi's thinking is important for Botta as well but the Italian-Swiss might have been even more directly influenced by Gregotti's theories, in which similar currents are also apparent, albeit with more pronounced Heideggerian undertones. Not only in his untranslated book *Il territorio dell'architettura* of 1966 but also in his later texts, such as the translated essay *Architecture, Environment, Nature,* Gregotti advocates formal architectonic interventions as instrument to reveal the essence of the context. The "constructed site" that Gregotti suggests is viewed as "the sum total of all things," physical (topographical) and non-physical (historical). Botta's affinities to such ideas are also apparent when Gregotti calls for the geometrical ordering of nature, therefore idealizing it.[6]

Mario Botta addresses his objections against what he sees as "static" and antiquarian kind of dealing with architecture's heritage by pointing to "a few big misunderstandings, that, today, subsist as generalized convictions." This is the section of the essay in which Botta describes intellectual misconceptions – he calls them "a very widespread attitude" and identifies environmental, landscape, and historical preservation and protection agencies

---

[6] Gregotti, Vittorio. "Architecture, Enviroment, Nature," in: Joan Ockman (ed.), *Architecture Culture.* New York: Rizzoli, 1993, p. 400.

as well as "a great many architects" as the main culprits – that prevent a commitment to continuously "finding a new balance between men and his ambient." Botta charges:

> "A misunderstanding that periodically re-emerges in the evaluation of the relationship between architecture and its ambient is the idea that subordinates every new architectonic intervention under a presumed superiority of the values of the preexisting context."

Here, Botta speaks about a habit that has been witnessed in hundreds of architecture schools almost everywhere around the globe ever since the concept of "contextualism" was introduced into the architectural discourse about a half of a century ago; and was misunderstood almost immediately. Even today – and maybe more so than ever before, due to such interests as environmentalism and sustainability that have infiltrated the architectural discourse – there are many misguided professors instructing their students to conduct site analyses in such a way that suggests and implies the value of the preexisting context as almost exclusively holding the secrets and limits for the new and yet-to-be projected architectonic intervention. Of course, it is needless to point out that this attitude decried by Botta is not just found in many architecture schools but is carried out to professional practice once these students leave the universities. Botta writes about this widespread attitude:

> *"In this perspective the territory is seen as the good that needs to be preserved and protected from the aggressions and the destructions inflicted by the new interventions."*

What Botta laments here is that in this perspective the architectonic act, the building that is to be projected and then to be built, is per definition viewed as something bad that destroys the supposedly good, the existing site that is. Botta further opposes that these various kinds of protection agencies and many architects interpret "the existing context and the environmental equilibrium as a static condition loaded with value" and he cheekingly points out that "these values are usually declared valuable and discovered for the first time just in time when a new architectonic intervention is imminent." Botta identifies this approach of architecture and the territory as "a reactionary attitude." He is merciless in his criticism of the "numerous protection and conservation commissions and societies" with their "most perverse aesthetical senses" when he further states that "the cultural corruption of these experts, judging by what has been produced in the last years, seems really not to have limits."

Rather than viewing the architectonic act as a reaction that is inherently understood as an act of lesser value imposed on an existing site of supposedly higher value, Botta defines a new architectonic act as a "fulcrum," a sort of a hinge that supports a transformation of the territory inevitably occurring as soon as men touch the building ground.

It is Botta's argument that it is exactly those protection and conservation agencies, having put in place building codes, of having failed to prevent hundreds of thousands of buildings of more than dubious architectural quality nor have these building codes "hindered speculative uses of the land for buildings." Rather, Botta argues, architectural quality is contingent on the strength of the "mutual and continuous exchange (giving-getting) ... between architecture and the ambient." Therefore, for Botta – and here we see his referencing the neo-rationalist approach against a timid and reactionary understanding of contextualism – "architecture is qualified as an instrument of construction of a new balance where the existing values will be considered – yet not defended or protected irrationally and overzealously – in order to be interpreted and projected as values for new needs." This is Botta's explanation of his understanding of each individual building as a "fulcrum." And making certain that the territory is not only understood as a physical fact but also as a fact that embodies a often long cultural heritage, Botta adds, "We should talk then not about protection but about promotion of the landscape's values and testimonies" in order "to finding a new balance between men and his ambient."

The criticism on the current condition addressed in this section of the essay is then followed with three programmatic "aspects" that Botta identifies as a sort of presupposition for his maxim of "[e]very work of architecture has its own ambient."

The first of Botta's aspects demands for "the reading and the interpretation of the ambient as a physical fact." Botta describes the "ambient as a physical fact" in the following way: "The territory is seen then as a place, a particular 'site,' something unique that is tightly linked to the geography and morphology of the context where we are called to work." According to Botta, architects are called upon to actively read and interpret those physical facts and not just to passively list and document them. The fact that Botta views even the reading and interpretation of the physical facts of the territory more so as an intellectual and artistic act than the mere act of accounting for each property of the site without hierarchy and judgment becomes clear when he calls "for comprehending and defining the identity of [a] place, for the identification of its meanings and its own peculiar characteristics, to adopt as elements of reference and continuous dialogue with the architectural fact."

If the first of the three programmatic aspects already implies a hefty artistic and intellectual-rational ability on part of the architect to make judgments about the ambient as a physical fact, then this is even more so the case for the second aspect. The second aspect is described as follows: "The second aspect is the ambient's interpretation, as evidenced in history and memory." He continues to refine his description with: "This is an aspect that involves all that exceeds physical facts." Botta lists what these non-physical facts entail: "symbolic aspects, atavic efforts, as well as unknown conflicts that the earth hides, which come back as memory's facts in every new project." In a beautiful sentence Botta ends his description of the second aspects with: "The ambient is also, and above all, evidence of the presence of men and of past generations that gives meaning and courage to our work."

Finally, the third aspect that Botta considers crucial for fulfilling the ambition of "[e]very architecture has its own ambient" is the presence of "the notion of time ... in the relations between architecture and the ambient." Botta asserts that architecture owns "the power to make a place different today from what and how it was yesterday." Contrary to the attempt of viewing the architectonic act as something fixated and arrested for eternity, Botta embraces buildings as "man-made artifices," values them as "the tangible expression of man's work," and ultimately views architecture as "a moment of continuous and dynamic reference with these 'cosmic' values of our life." Therefore, according to Botta's view, it is not only the architectonic act that changes everything around itself but it also changes itself. In Botta's own words we read: "In this way architecture is changing and transforming itself in synchronization with its time."

Botta ends his essay by reaffirming that it requires the "comparison and awareness of these facts," just listed above, with which architecture "can be fed by its context" and much less so through the often thoughtless, inartistic, and irrational "illusions and phantoms of an impossible conservation." Rather than value the nostalgic mimicry of the past, Botta defines "ARCHITECTURE AS A FORMAL EXPRESSION OF HISTORY" and such architecture "will know how to be an active witness of the aspirations, of the concerns, and of the hopes of our culture."

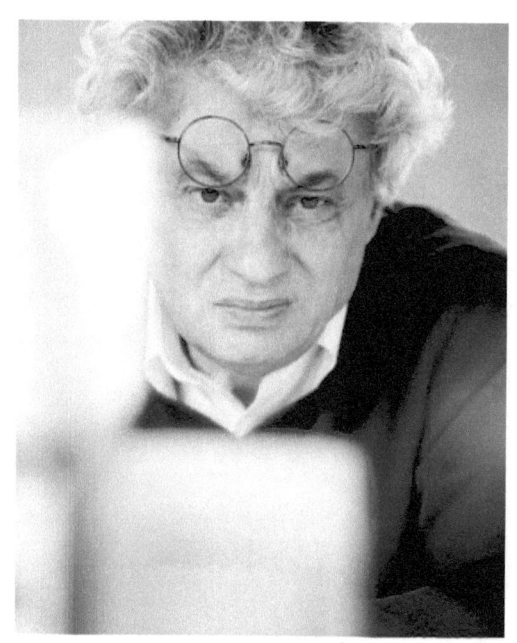

MARIO BOTTA
ARCHITECT

BIOGRAPHICAL INFORMATION

MARIO BOTTA was born on April 1, 1943 in Mendrisio, located in the Canton of Ticino, the Italian-speaking region of Switzerland. His family is from the nearby town of Genestrerio. From 1958 to 1961, Mario Botta learns the craft of an architecture draughtsman in the office of Carloni & Camenisch in Lugano, Switzerland, and then attends a lyceum of the arts in Milano, Italy, from 1961 to 1964. The baccalurean education is followed by the study of architecture at the *Istituto Universitario di Architettura (IUAV)* in Venice, Italy, from 1964 to 1969. Botta's thesis advisors are Carlo Scarpa and Giuseppe Mazzariol. Architects, historians, theoreticians, and critics such as Aldo Rossi, Manfredo Tafuri, and Vittorio Gregotti belong to the loosely associated so-called "School of Venice" which intellectually stimulates the rich architectural discourse at the IUAV at the time and are also known collectively as the *La Tendenza*. Botta works as an architecture intern in the office of Le Corbusier in 1965 and, after meeting Louis Kahn in Venice, is involved with the preparation for Kahn's exhibition of a new project. Mario Botta establishes his own architecture office in Lugano in 1970 but by that point in time he already had projected a two-family house for his family in Morbio Superiore, Switzerland, at the youthful age of sixteen, a rectory in his hometown Genestrerio from 1961 to 1963, as well as a house in Stabio from 1965 to 1966, the latter conceived as an homage for Le Corbusier. A series of masterly buildings in the Ticino region such as the house in Cadenazzo (1970 to 1971), a house in Riva San Vitale (1972 to 1973), a school in Morbio Inferiore (1972 to 1977) and a series of competition projects for a school in Locarno, Switzerland (1970), the master plan for the Federal Swiss Institute of Technology in Lausanne, Switzerland (1970), and for an administration center in Perugia, Italy (1971), elevate Botta's position as one of the seminal architects of a loosely associated group of *Ticino*-based architects who aim to reconsider anew the presuppositions of architecture in the late 1960s and early 1970s. The work of these *Ticino*-based architects first receive national and international recognition by means of an exhibition titled *Tendenzen – Neuere Architektur im Tessin [Tendenza* – Recent Architecture in Ticino], held at the Swiss Federal Institute of Technology (ETH) in Zurich in November 1975. Other important architects of the rather heterogeneous work shown at the exhibition were Peppo Brivio, Alberto Camenzind, Mario Campi, Tita Carloni, Aurelio Galfetti, Augusto Jäggli, Franco Pessina, Carlo Ponti, Bruno Reichlin, Fabio Reinhart, Flora Ruchat, Dolf Schnebli, Luigi Snozzi, Rino Tami, Ivo Trümpy, and Livio Vacchini. Based on the title of the influential exhibition, these architects were labeled as the *Ticino Tendenza,* and Mario Botta would become their internationally most successful exponent. A common denominator of the *Ticino Tendenza* is described in the exhibition catalogue by exhibition curator Martin Steinmann with the following words: "… a clear preconception on the relationship of architecture with its external conditions, but also the recognition of architecture as a discipline which owns its own internal laws, in other words, the autonomy of architecture." The catalogue also contains Mario Botta's most influential statement he has made on architecture: "The architectonic intervention is not an opportunity to build AT A PLACE but the artifact to BUILD A

PLACE, inasmuch as architecture becomes a part within a new geographic configuration that owns an irresolvable connection with the value of history and the memory of a place and, therefore, is a expression and attest of aspirations and values of contemporary culture." The short essay translated in this volume speaks directly to this statement on architecture. The success of the exhibition at the ETH leads to an encompassing dossier in the prominent Japanese architecture journal *Architecture + Urbanism (a+u)* and, as a consequence of that publication, worldwide exposure less than one year after the exhibition in Zurich. The *a+u* dossier subsequently becomes a reference for the British architecture historian Kenneth Frampton to point to the work of the *Ticino Tendenza,* and the buildings of Mario Botta specifically, as an important component in Frampton's construct of *Critical Regionalism* (the concept was originally introduced into architecture theoretical debate in slightly different meaning by Alexander Tzonis and Liane Lefaivre) in his essay *Towards a Critical Regionalism: Six points for an architecture of resistance* published in Hal Foster's compilation *Anti-Aesthetic. Essays on Postmodern Culture* in 1983.

Botta and his architecture's international importance reached its apex by means of being included
as an important example in a new chapter titled
*Postscript 1983: Modern Architecture and Critical
Regionalism* in the extended 1983 German edition
of Frampton's landmark publication *Modern Architecture. A Critical History*. As a consequence of
those debates and publications, Mario Botta was
one of the most discussed and most prominent architects worldwide of the early 1980s and his work
is thus indelibly linked with the architectural debates surrounding "place," "critical regionalism,"
"postmodern culture" and "postmodern architecture." Mario Botta began to lecture at architecture
schools around the world, and he eventually re-
ceived many commissions for buildings in Switzerland and around the world from 1979 onward.
Some of his best know buildings are: a house in
Pregassona, Switzerland (1979), a house in Stabio,
Switzerland (1980), the Banca del Gottardo in Lugano, Switzerland (1982), San Francisco Museum
of Modern Art, San Francisco (1994), a cathedral
in Evry outside of Paris (1995), the Church of San
Giovanni Battista in Mogno, Switzerland (1996),
and the Casino di Campione, located in an Italian

enclave in Switzerland (2007). Mario Botta held his first visiting professorship at the Swiss Federal Institute of Technology in Lausanne in 1979. This appointment was followed by many other academic and professional engagements around the world that continue to this day. Mario Botta has been awarded with many international prizes, awards, and recognitions. Mario Botta owns a pivotal role in the establishment of the *Accedemia di Architettura* at the *Università della Svizzera Italiana* in Mendrisio, where he is currently on his second tenure as dean of the school.

Text: Markus Breitschmid

ALICE FRANCESCONI is an architecture student from Aosta, Italy. She studies architecture at the Accademia di Architettura of the Università della Svizzera Italiana in Mendrisio, Switzerland.

MARIANNA GIULIA GALBUSERA is an architecture student from Milano, Italy. She studies architecture at the Accademia di Architettura of the Università della Svizzera Italiana in Mendrisio, Switzerland.

MARKUS BREITSCHMID is a trained architect, theoretician, and author on architecture from Lucerne, Switzerland. He obtained his doctorate from the Technische Universität Berlin. He currently is a professor at Virginia Polytechnic Institute & State University in Blacksburg, Virginia.

PHOTOGRAPHIC CREDITS

Photographs of buildings depicted in this volume were taken by Markus Breitschmid. The portrait photograph of Mario Botta is not attributed.

TEXTS ON ARCHITECTURE AND ART
A SERIES OF VIRGINIA TECH ARCHITECTURE PUBLICATIONS
MARKUS BREITSCHMID, EDITOR OF SERIES

In Print:

Julius Meier-Graefe. A Modern Milieu [1901] 2007
Edited and Texts by Markus Breitschmid
Translation by Harry Francis Mallgrave & Markus Breitschmid
ISBN 978-0-9794296-0-6

Mario Botta. Architecture and the Ambient [ca. 1983] 2013
Edited and Texts by Markus Breitschmid
Translation by Alice Francesconi and Marianna Galbusera with the
Assistance of Markus Breitschmid
ISBN: 978-0-9893936-5-2

In Preparation:

Alfred Lichtwark. Realist Architecture [1899]
Edited by Markus Breitschmid
Translation by Harry Francis Mallgrave & Markus Breitschmid

Hermann Muthesius. New Ornament and New Art [1901]
Edited by Markus Breitschmid
Translation by Harry Francis Mallgrave & Markus Breitschmid

Fritz Schumacher. Style and Fashion [1889, 1902]
Edited by Markus Breitschmid
Translation by Harry Francis Mallgrave & Markus Breitschmid

Virginia Tech Architecture Publications
Blacksburg, Virginia 24061-0205
United States of America
Phone: +1-540-231-5383
www.archdesign.vt.edu

www.ingramcontent.com/pod-product-compliance
Lightning Source LLC
Chambersburg PA
CBHW021008180526
45163CB00005B/1929